OPEN UP
Her WORLD

SHENIADA JOHNSON

Copyright © 2022 Sheniada Johnson

ALL RIGHTS RESERVED.

This book contains material protected under International and Federal Copyright Laws and Treaties. Any unauthorized reprint or use of this material is prohibited. No part of this book may be reproduced or transmitted in any form or by any means, electronic or mechanical, including photocopying, recording, or by any information storage and retrieval system without express written permission from the author/publisher.

Unless otherwise noted, all scripture quotations are taken from the King James Version of the Bible. All rights reserved.

Scripture is taken from the New King James Version®. Copyright © 1982 by Thomas Nelson. All rights reserved.

Scripture quotations taken from the (NASB®) New American Standard Bible®, Copyright © 2020 by The Lockman Foundation. Used by permission. All rights reserved. www.lockman.org

Scripture quotations are from the ESV® Bible (The Holy Bible, English Standard Version®), copyright © 2001 by Crossway, a publishing ministry of Good News Publishers. Used by permission. All rights reserved.

American Bible Society. (1976). *Good News Bible: The Bible in Today's English version.* New York: American Bible Society.

Book Cover Design: Prize Publishing House

Printed by: Prize Publishing House, LLC in the United States of America.

First printing edition 2022.

Prize Publishing House
P.O. Box 9856, Chesapeake, VA 23321
www.PrizePublishingHouse.com

ISBN (Paperback): 978-1-7379751-9-9
ISBN (E-Book): 979-8-9858926-0-4

Library of Congress Control Number: 2022904606

CONTENTS

INTRODUCTION..v

SECTION 1: FELLOWSHIP

DAY 1:   LOST IN RELIGIOUSNESS WITHOUT LIFE.............1
DAY 2:   LIMITED BY RELIGIOUS NORMS 5
DAY 3:   GOD IS INTERESTED IN YOU 7
DAY 4:   GOD IS CALLING YOU 11
DAY 5:   FOUND TRUE WORSHIP 13

SECTION 2: REJECTION

DAY 6:   SOCIETAL REJECTION 19
DAY 7:   JILTED BY A PARTNER 21
DAY 8:   PARENTAL ABANDONMENT 23
DAY 9:   GOD'S OPEN ARMS 25

SECTION 3: HEALING

DAY 10: GOD CAN FIX IT (PHYSICAL HEALING).............29
DAY 11: HEALING INSIDE-OUT (EMOTIONAL HEALING) 31
DAY 12: OVERCOMING ADDICTION (SPIRITUAL HEALING).....33
DAY 13: MOVING FORWARD 35

SECTION 4: FORGIVENESS

DAY 14: IS THERE A SECOND CHANCE WITH GOD? 39
DAY 15: FORGIVING YOURSELF (LET IT GO)................41
DAY 16: FORGIVING OTHERS 43

SECTION 5: IDENTITY

- DAY 17: WHOSE REPORT WILL YOU BELIEVE? (WHAT SOCIETY THINKS OF WOMEN, YOU OR GOD)...47
- DAY 18: WHO ARE YOU IN CHRIST? (FINDING SELF) 51
- DAY 19: WHAT'S THE ESSENCE OF YOUR EXISTENCE?........................53

SECTION 6: FREEDOM

- DAY 20: NO MORE CONDEMNATION 57
- DAY 21: NO MORE LIMITATIONS..59
- DAY 22: LAUNCH THE WOMAN IN YOU..61
- DAY 23: LAUNCH YOUR POTENTIAL..63
- DAY 24: LAUNCH THE LEADER IN YOU..65
- DAY 25: REACH FOR THE STARS 67

SECTION 7: THE LOVE OF GOD

- DAY 26: HOW DEEP IS THE FATHER'S LOVE?..................................71
- DAY 27: GOD'S LOVE NEVER FAILS 73
- DAY 28: HIS BANNER OVER YOU IS LOVE......................................75
- DAY 29: GOD'S LOVE IS PATIENT...77
- DAY 30: GOD'S LOVE IS EVERLASTING..81

CONCLUSION 85

INTRODUCTION

It's such a wonderful time to learn about us as ladies of quite essential value. The best we can discover about ourselves can only be found in God. As we set out on a 30-day journey of self-discovery, I strongly believe you will be enlightened and empowered to step out to the world and shine forth the light of God. I am sure you are as excited as I am already.

Before we begin, let me introduce you briefly to the *Open Up Her World* movement by sharing a few of my personal experiences with you.

Open Up Her World is designed to help you see your world through relationship and not religion. It is of utmost importance to God, even as it benefits us, to have and maintain an intimate relationship with God, our Father, for ourselves, and for only Jesus Himself. He never meant that we only know Him through performance or having fun at church. God is a spirit, and those who worship Him, communicating with or having an intimate relationship with Him, must do so in spirit and truth, not in vain and unproductive traditions or forms of piety. Through years of common practice, many of you have been programmed to believe in the God of the Bible; only your pastor knows Him or can talk to Him. Week after week, we inflate to go out on the same day at the start of the week with the same old behavior, attitude, thought, or action. Without a minute, an hour, or a day to pray, read the Bible, or spend time with God for ourselves. I've done this myself for a long time, missing out for years, I felt. I will not overstate that this took 30 years of my life. I remember it was like going to church on Sunday, studying the Bible on Tuesday, and other services like conferences, revivals, or prayer meetings. The thought came maybe I was running away from something or someone, looking for something or someone. I realize now I was just there all the time when the church doors were open, as they say in the Christian community, like I had no job and no family. I was at these services and just sat as no one even noticed me for many years. As I did this week after week, I thought I was doing the right thing, and that's all I knew.

As a little girl, I remember sitting in the front row of the church. I went to school every day and came home; as far as I can remember, this was the summary of my routine. How did I go from this shy, naive, scary, simple, lonely, and quiet girl to womanhood? I want to share my spiritual path from a mere religious act or a form of piety to a truly intimate relationship with God. My life would be a different story if I were not bored with the old routine; if I had not realized by saying, "God, there must be more," when I had not seen the truth of God's word, or I had not tried to find out for myself about Him. Right now, I can't imagine what my life would be like. I don't have a perfect retrospective of what I missed initially when I accepted Jesus Christ as my Savior. I have questioned my salvation many times, leading me to reiterate my acceptance of Jesus Christ as my Lord and Savior. At first, I didn't fully understand what it meant or what it meant to be a believer. Life around me was only happening to me, but I had no clue truthfully. I have spent a lot of time trying to build personal relationships with other people. Now that I'm on the relationship side, it's easy to identify other people who are passing through these same issues and offer enlightenment.

Early in my transformation, God revealed things in a way that I understood. How did He know that I would understand what message

He was trying to convey to me, be it in a song, His word, or even a dream? I started to see more clearly, and my mind became more aware since I entered this beautiful relationship with God the Father, and it is no longer just a religion. I discovered impressive and beautiful things about myself and the world I live in today.

In the same way, this devotional will help you open your world to several possibilities of God and enjoy the essence of your life as a woman of God.

Section One

FELLOWSHIP

Day 1

LOST IN RELIGIOUSNESS WITHOUT LIFE

"Now it happened as they went that He entered a certain village; and a certain woman named Martha welcomed Him into her house. And she had a sister called Mary, who also sat at Jesus' feet and heard His word. But Martha was distracted with much serving, and she approached Him and said, "Lord, do You not care that my sister has left me to serve alone? Therefore tell her to help me." And Jesus answered and said to her, "Martha, Martha, you are worried and troubled about many things. But one thing is needed, and Mary has chosen that good part, which will not be taken away from her."

LUKE 10:38-42, NKJV

Do you practice religion, or do you have a real relationship with Jesus Christ? When you pray, does your heart seek Christ? What's a relationship without intimacy? Is your prayer life boring? If so, then this is solid proof that you are leaning towards religion.

When I came across this scripture again several months ago, I gained a new understanding different from the usual and casual way I have perceived this scripture. Suddenly, I realized I had played the role of Martha for so long. I was lost in religious activities without having any personal experience of who Jesus is.

Many times believers are deceived by the many meetings and conferences they attend and forget the place of personal communication with God. Martha was a devoted follower of Christ, just like we have devoted churchgoers in our present-day churches. Many have lost touch with God, and the devil has successfully blinded their hearts from experiencing God personally.

What the church needs at this perilous time is Christians like Mary. God needs Christians who will abstain from religious activities and focus on Him alone. At the end of our race, what will remain important is how much of God we have personally experienced and given expression to, not the number of religious activities and meetings we have attended.

Religion can easily dominate your prayer life. Religion can easily dominate your daily walk with Christ. Religion paralyzes your relationship with God and hinders you greatly. Believers go as far as using "religious excuses" to live in rebellion and worldliness. We must be careful not to harden our hearts to correction.

God wants relationship! He doesn't want you to try to be religious. He wants you to find Him. Words are meaningless if the heart is wrong.

They said, "I spent an hour in prayer today. I did my duty." No! Prayer is not work. This is joy. It is a privilege to be in the presence of Almighty God! Of course, we regard prayer as work if we do it out of obligation, not out of love. I believe that more than 75% of the faithful do not actually pray.

One great hymn-writer said, "I often say my prayers. But have I ever prayed? And do the desires of my heart go hand in hand with the words I speak?" I can also kneel and worship the stone god and pray to the living God with only words. For God will never hear words without the heart, nor will He be present on lips whose prayers are not sincere.

Lord, teach me what I need and teach me to pray; Also, don't allow me to ask for your mercy without feeling what I'm saying.

1. Enough of any religious activity without focusing on God.
2. It is now time to sit at the feet of the Master to learn of Him.
3. I desire a personal experience of God.

Day 2

LIMITED BY RELIGIOUS NORMS

"Let your women keep silent in the churches, for they are not permitted to speak; but they are to be submissive, as the law also says."

1 Corinthians 14:34, NKJV

Religion is often seen as an obstacle to gender equality. There are many stories of gender-based violence perpetrated in the name of religion. As a result, in many cases, religion and gender inclusion issues are considered too complex. There seems to be no way to break this rather complicated issue.

In Christianity, several New Testament texts are quoted to deny women the right to be priests and pastors for much of its history. Mind you, we are not in any way making a case for gender equality with this book.

However, many have misinterpreted the above scripture by relegating women to the background in the church. Women's creative voices and ideas are silenced during vital and productive meetings.

While personally studying this scripture, it suddenly dawned on me that the Jewish Law is not Jesus' Law. While Jesus was on earth doing ministry, He never silenced the voice of anyone irrespective of their gender.

Instead of generally seeing women as inferior or incapable of leadership, women should be seen as "equal to the task."

It's high time the church embraced the important role and impact women can have in God's kingdom. Jesus came for both male and female. God can use both the male and the female gender.

1. I can no longer be restricted to the back.
2. My voice will be heard loud and strong for God.
3. I am useful in God's kingdom. God wants to use me. I am ready to be used by God.

Day 3

GOD IS INTERESTED IN YOU

"Are not two sparrows sold for a copper coin? And not one of them falls to the ground apart from your Father's will. But the very hairs of your head are all numbered. Do not fear therefore; you are of more value than many sparrows.."

MATTHEW 10:29-31, NKJV

God is interested in you as a woman. I have been in a dire situation where I was confused on so many issues surrounding whether I was loved and useful to God. Some church assemblies make you feel not so loved by God or make you feel ostracized out of God's plan.

In my search for answers, God drew my attention to this scripture. God reassured me of how deep His interests are over my life and every other woman out there. I was brought to examine how God cared for the beasts of the air. If God could show unimaginable love and interest in the birds of the air, how much more interest will He have over me whom He created in His image and likeness.

He didn't stop there. He went as far as saying that He took out time to count and number the very hairs of my head! Wow! This is massive.

I don't know who else has enough patience and interest to number all the hairs on my head.

Let no man deceive you; God is interested in you. Don't allow any religious law or church doctrines to deprive you of the blessings which come in the awareness of God's special interest in you.

God cares for you more than you think. Letting His only Son die for you shows that you've caught His eye, so stop reaching out to Him like you're a necessary evil stealing His precious time for more important things.

The thoughts He has for you are for good, not evil, to give you the goals you so desire and DESERVE. He says that you must boldly come to His Seat of Mercy for help when you need it. He said that He is your Father, and you are His sons, and if you ask for fish, He will not give you a snake, and if you ask for bread, He will not give you a stone. He says He knows how to give you good gifts, and if you trust Him, you will never be ashamed.

He says He will support, strengthen and beautify you. He will make you the joy of many nations, and kings will come in the splendor of your majesty. See, you will eventually overcome this situation because He made you more of a conqueror through Christ.

So, the next time you go to Him, enter into His presence with song and into His courts with praise with all boldness, for the Creator of heaven and earth, the Mighty One, Alpha and Omega, the One, before whom the mountains are.

If God cares about us, then every part of our life is important to God. And because God's divine energy is limitless, God's interest in us doesn't come and go. He is always there for us. Therefore, it makes sense to seek God with all our heart, thank God with deep gratitude for God's grace, and ask God for help when we are in darkness and pain.

We seek, with all our heart, a divine friendship that never fails because God's interest in us never dies.

If you are not yet His child, then you are missing out on the best paternal love in the entire universe. All you must do is believe that this great Father sent His only Son to die for you. He shed His blood for you as payment for your sins, and on the third day, He rose from the dead so that you too can be a part of this big family. Accept Jesus as your Lord and Savior in your heart and confess with your mouth that He is Lord of your life and start this great journey with this family.

1. I can't be intimidated any longer! I am loved by God.
2. God is so much interested in me. He cares for me.
3. I am worth more than many sparrows.

Day 4

GOD IS CALLING YOU

"Behold, I stand at the door and knock. If anyone hears My voice and opens the door, I will come in to him and dine with him, and he with Me."

REVELATIONS 3:20, NKJV

Many ladies out here feel that God cannot call them, or God doesn't need a woman in ministry. I am here to categorically announce that God is standing at the door of your heart, and He is knocking, calling out your name.

God's calling is not gender-based, neither is God unjust in His dealings. Many churches and Christian organizations have successfully brainwashed the female gender to believe God can't call them. Society has also relegated womanhood to the kitchen and to a sex machine. Meanwhile, in the scripture above, God said if **anyone** hears Him calling and opens the door, He will come in and interact with the person.

That scripture does not indicate or reveal any particular gender; therefore, God can call anyone.

God is the Creator of all things, and His creative vision is big enough to involve women from all social classes, from diverse backgrounds and cultures. His eternal goals span several generations. His will was large enough to include young virgins like the praying Rhoda and virgins like Mary, the young mother of Jesus. The plans were big enough for women like Elizabeth, Rachel, and Hannah, all of whom had long been barren. His destinations included women with pagan backgrounds like Ruth, prostitutes like Rahab and the outcasts, widows, and adulterous women like the Samaritan woman at the well. He saw marginalized and enslaved women like Hagar and older women like the prophet Anna. He embraces women like this with compassion because His purpose and plan include them all. God's purposes include you!

I want you to begin to embrace every possibility of God calling you in every sphere of life. Whether in your career, business, or academics, God is calling you to stand for Him.

More than ever before, God is calling you as an individual into a personal relationship and fellowship with Him. He said if anyone hears His voice and opens up to Him, He will come and fellowship with the person. This is a call into fellowship with God.

1. I will answer the call of God over my life.
2. I will open up the door of my heart for a personal fellowship with God.
3. Henceforth, I enjoy intimacy with my Lord.

Day 5

FOUND TRUE WORSHIP

> *"'These people draw near to Me with their mouth, And honor Me with their lips, But their heart is far from Me. And in vain they worship Me, Teaching as doctrines the commandments of men.'"*
> — MATT 15:8-9, NKJV

> *"But the hour is coming, and now is, when the true worshipers will worship the Father in spirit and truth; for the Father is seeking such to worship Him. God is Spirit, and those who worship Him must worship in spirit and truth."*
> — JOHN 4:23-24, NKJV

I have been in church for many years and have seen people come into the church to worship God and, after that, go back to their homes to begin living life practically outside the will and dictates of God.

I couldn't understand how people would confess a thing today and do the exact opposite in the next minute. No wonder Jesus said that many people worship from the lips, but their hearts are very far away from Him.

I have come to understand that true worship comes from the heart of a believer. If everything we do and profess does not come from our sincere heart towards God, then all we do is in vain.

The fourth chapter of the book of John reveals that the time and hour comes when true worshippers will arise to begin to offer sincere incense of worship to God. God has always been searching for true worshippers who will worship Him in spirit and in truth.

Worshiping in spirit means worshiping from the heart or from within. This is different from formal, ceremonial, outward worship by those whose hearts are not with God (Matthew 15:8). Therefore, the most important factor in becoming a devotee is maintaining and cultivating the heart for God. Worship in the spirit is faith in the heart that produces prayer, purity of conscience, and self-denial that leads to obedience.

Jesus told this woman that the great transition was at hand (4:23): *"But the time is coming, and now is the time when the true worshiper will worship the Father in spirit and in truth."* The presence of Jesus initiated this change from the Old Testament to the New Testament. In the old way of worship, the place was important: all Jewish men had to appear before God for the three annual feasts in Jerusalem (Deuteronomy 16:16). But in a new way that Jesus found, He is a new temple (John 2:19-21). Believers are built up in temples in the Lord (Ephesians 2:21; 1 Peter 2:5). Therefore, the place where we gather to worship is secondary. How and who we worship is fundamental.

Like the Samaritan women of the time, unbelievers often mistakenly believed that things were right between them and God when they went through the externals of "worship." When they go to the church building and go through the weekly services, they think everything is fine. But they don't worship God from their heart. They have not repented of their sins in thought, word, or deed. So, Jesus told him that the outside was not as important as the inside. We must make it our priority to become true worshipers of God in spirit and in truth.

I believe that worship in spirit is partly emotional or felt. That doesn't mean we have to pump up our emotions with music or crowds. True emotions about God arise when we focus our minds on the truth about who He is and what He did for us on the cross. But if your worship never touches your emotions, something is wrong. It's like a relationship with a lover. My relationship with Him was not based on my feelings but on my devotion to Him. But when I think about all that He means to me, I feel love for Him, and I must express that love externally to show Him that I love Him.

A Declaration

1. It is time for me to worship from my heart in all sincerity.
2. I will worship God in spirit and in truth.
3. Enough of pretense. God cannot be mocked.

Section Two

REJECTION

Day 6

SOCIETAL REJECTION

"If the world hates you, you know that it hated Me before it hated you. If you were of the world, the world would love its own. Yet because you are not of the world, but I chose you out of the world, therefore the world hates you. Remember the word that I said to you, 'A servant is not greater than his master.' If they persecuted Me, they will also persecute you. If they kept My word, they will keep yours also. But all these things they will do to you for My name's sake, because they do not know Him who sent Me. If I had not come and spoken to them, they would have no sin, but now they have no excuse for their sin. [23] He who hates Me hates My Father also. If I had not done among them the works which no one else did, they would have no sin; but now they have seen and also hated both Me and My Father. But this happened that the word might be fulfilled which is written in their law, 'They hated Me without a cause.'"

— JOHN 15:18-25, NKJV

We live in a world where women constantly receive messages that convey that they are not worthy. You are not smart enough for this job or capable enough to make that kind of money. You're not skinny enough to fit in these jeans. You're not attractive enough to date this person or have a guy who is wholly dedicated just to you. You are not competent enough to be a leader. You are not a great parent. You are not a wonderful wife. And when we feel insecure or inadequate, it's easy to embarrass or disapprove of women who are more confident than us or who have made choices other than us. This rejection makes us somehow feel better and more comfortable with our decisions, even if only for a moment.

This is a clear indication that we would constantly face rejection in this world because we do not belong to this corrupt world.

As Christians, the world is persecuting us. Much more because you are a woman of difference and with a passionate love for God, the world will persecute and avoid having any serious association with you.

There is a popular saying that if you want everyone to be happy with you, you have to become a man-pleaser. That is exactly what the world wants. You have to do what society loves to be loved by society.

Because we don't live our life to please the world, they will reject us for who we are and what we stand for. Jesus, our maker, was faced with rejection from those He came to save. In the same manner, we might face rejection from those to whom we have shown nothing but love and care. When this happens, take it with a good heart and continue doing well.

1. I will keep doing well whether the world accepts me or not.
2. The world might reject me; my God will never reject me. I am satisfied.

Day 7

JILTED BY A PARTNER

"Have I not commanded you? Be strong and of good courage; do not be afraid, nor be dismayed, for the Lord your God is with you wherever you go."

— Joshua 1:9, NKJV —

Breakups can be tough, no matter the circumstances. Everyone feels differently when experiencing a breakup. It's good to be sad, angry, or frustrated after a breakup - lots of people do!

Sometimes you need to prioritize taking care of yourself, and there are things you can do to make things easier. You need to do things like go out with friends, eat healthily, and get lots of sleep.

It's good to be sad after a breakup, and it takes time to get over the loss of a relationship.

After a breakup, many people experience various difficult feelings, such as sadness, anger, or guilt, which can lead to feelings of rejection, confusion, or loneliness. You may even feel relieved, which can be just as confusing.

Some people feel the world has turned upside down, and things will never be right again. Many people may feel restless, lose their appetite, and lack the motivation or energy to do something. Breaking up quickly may be tempting, but it takes a little time, work, and support.

But here is God saying to you, "Be strong and courageous." He said, don't be discouraged; He has promised to stand by you through it all.

Don't entertain any suicidal thoughts or any depressing energy that might rob you of your potential. You are more than this. You are not without a comforter.

1. I am encouraged by God. Nothing can weigh me down.
2. God is preparing the best partner for me.
3. I take every disappointment as a blessing in disguise.

Day 8

PARENTAL ABANDONMENT

"Can a woman forget her nursing child, And not have compassion on the son of her womb? Surely they may forget, Yet I will not forget you."

Isaiah 49:15, NKJV

"When my father and my mother forsake me, then the Lord will take me up."

Psalm 27:10, KJV

I know it might be difficult to believe and phantom the fact of the possibility of a parent abandoning a child that they have trained and spent hugely on. However, that is the reality we experience today.

Across the nations of the earth, we see teens and young adults who have been disowned by their parents owing to one issue or the other. The prevalence of abandoned babies in orphanage homes keeps increasing at an alarming rate.

Isaiah helps us see the possibility of a breastfeeding mother forgetting her baby and refusing to show compassion by caring for the baby. How much more a grown individual?

Your parents or guardian can abandon you at any moment in life. They can refuse to support or show compassion no matter how little it could be. They are all human, and humans can disappoint you at the least expected moments of your life.

Isaiah also reveals where we can find a safe haven when facing parental denial or abandonment. Isaiah said, "Though she may forget, God will not forget." Herein lays a great revelation. God will never abandon us!

King David also had this revelation that God shows up to uphold him when his father and mother often forsake him in the bush.

Likewise, whenever you are faced with abandonment, and your parents have relinquished their responsibilities on you, remember God, who is much more interested in you, will never forsake you. He will hold you up by His right hand.

A Declaration

1. God can never abandon me. I am loved by God.
2. When my parent abandons me, I will pick myself up in the Lord and move forward.
3. I am God's own delight. My heavenly Father will uphold me.

Day 9

GOD'S OPEN ARMS

"All that the Father gives Me will come to Me, and the one who comes to Me I will [f]by no means cast out."

— JOHN 6:37, NKJV

"Let us, therefore, come boldly unto the throne of grace that we may obtain mercy and find grace to help in time of need."

— HEBREWS 4:16, KJV

Years ago, I was of the opinion that God's arms are not open to everyone. Maybe because of my experiences while growing up thinking God is partial to who He loves and relates to well.

I saw God working intimately in some people's lives and saw some people who looked like total strangers to God. You could say my eyes were deceiving me. However, I never knew God's arms were wide open to everyone.

You know, sometimes we are slow and reluctant to go to God, thinking He won't accept us. We look at our load of sins and errors; we look at our failures and inabilities and suddenly feel God's definition of His vessel is far from us. In Isaiah 1:18, He said, *"Come now, and let us reason together, said the Lord……"* Can you see that? God's arms are open to everyone irrespective of gender, race, and nationality. His arms are wide open to you. All you need is to decide to walk in.

Go before Him in prayer; pour out your mind before Him. Get naked before your maker. Let Him know how you've failed and disappointed Him. Let Him know how inadequate you are in yourself. Build a very strong intimacy with Him; romance the Holy Spirit and enjoy His presence. Let God pour Himself on you. Indeed, His arms are wide open. Are you ready?

1. I will daily run to my lover (God).
2. Daily, will I boldly show up before the throne of grace.
3. I have access to God every day and every time.

Section Three

HEALING

Day 10

GOD CAN FIX IT (PHYSICAL HEALING)

"Behold, I will bring it health and healing; I will heal them and reveal to them the abundance of peace and truth."

— JEREMIAH 33:6, NKJV

Are you experiencing any form of infirmity that has constantly preyed on your health, and for so long, you have searched for healing, and the doctors could not trace the cause, nor could they offer a solution to the ailment? God is the greatest physician, and no ailment is above His power.

You can run to God for that healing you so desire. God can fix it. Is there anything God can't do? Certainly not! He can fix that seemingly terminal illness in your life. Indeed, God can.

Six years ago, I got perfectly healed of breast cancer after battling it for several years. I became afraid at some point, thinking I wasn't going to survive it. But you know what? I simply answered NO to Jeremiah 32:27. There's nothing God cannot do; in fact, what God can't do doesn't exist.

You probably have heard or seen people healed of deadly diseases and terminal illnesses. God is still in the business of doing the same. Don't allow that sickness or physical challenges to reduce you to nothing or send you to your early grave. Get determined to allow God's Word to prevail in your life.

We were told Jesus healed all manners of sicknesses, including mental health challenges. I don't know what that situation is in your life, woman of God, but God can fix it. I don't care to know how long you've cried; God can fix it. They may have ridiculed you on account of it; God can fix it. The Master is set to wipe out your shame completely and rewrite your story. He made the body; He can replace any worn-out part.

God alone is the Master healer, tested and trusted. Allow Him to fix yours today!

1. I submit myself at the feet of God for my healing.
2. God will bring health and healing my way today/
3. Only God can fix it all for me.

Day 11

HEALING INSIDE-OUT (EMOTIONAL HEALING)

> *"The LORD is near to those who have a broken heart,*
> *And saves such as have a contrite spirit."*
> — PSALMS 34:18, NKJV

> *"Come to Me, all you who labor and are heavy*
> *laden, and I will give you rest."*
> — MATTHEW 11:28, NKJV

We live in a culture flooded with psychotherapy, counseling programs, treatment centers, mental hospitals, antidepressants, recovery support groups, books, videos, and podcasts. Many of them are amazing and save lives.

But we also live in a country that is among the worst in the world for poor emotional health. There's a huge gap, isn't there? Perhaps you are in this abyss, tired of your emotional pain and wondering how to heal it.

To be clear, I strongly believe that some people who suffer from emotional distress could benefit from professional help. However, sometimes we try to cope with the symptoms and stop dealing with the source of the pain. God will get to the heart of the matter with the recipe I want to offer you. You will be surprised by its simplicity.

> *"Is anyone among you suffering? Let him pray.."*
> — JAMES 5:13. —

The word "suffering" here means anxiety, stress, and despair. Have you ever felt like this? Of course, we all have.

But here is God saying He is close to the brokenhearted and is ever willing to minister healing to the brokenhearted.

Sometimes God chooses to bring healing right away. I believe we will see an increase in this type of healing. For those struggling with emotional health, keep pushing for a healing miracle; God has this for you. Realize, too, that your healing can be a journey like mine was. Also, embark on a path that can include layers of healing and freedom. Emotional wounds are deep, and sometimes our healing journey is like peeling the layers of an onion.

1. I receive healing for my broken heart.
2. I am empowered to let go of everything that has caused me to hurt.
3. I receive the beginning of a new dawn.

Day 12

OVERCOMING ADDICTION (SPIRITUAL HEALING)

"No temptation has overtaken you except such as is common to man, but God is faithful, who will not allow you to be tempted beyond what you are able, but with the temptation will also make the way of escape, that you may be able to bear it."

1 Corinthians 10:13, NKJV

Dear friend, are you stuck in addiction and struggling to get rid of it? It doesn't matter what kind of addiction. The first addiction begins as relaxation, entertainment, or to satisfy curiosity. Addiction to masturbation and pornography, for example, arises from the lust of the opposite sex. Gambling can be started as fun and games. An early win can force a person to aim for the next win. But the losses can soon outweigh the initial gains. Many return to gambling to win back lost money.

Hear this; if you are stuck in an addiction, you need to find the source of the addiction and deal with it immediately. Do you intend to make more money quickly from gambling? Do you secretly want the opposite sex and become sexually addicted? Do you think you can find peace with alcohol and drugs? Neither of these addictions will bring peace. The fun will soon be over, and the pain of addiction will soon be over. Guilt, debt, and health problems arise as addiction persists.

God can help us overcome. The Bible says: *"Behold, the hand of the Lord is not too short to save, nor is His ear too dull to hear. But your sins have separated you from your Lord; your sins hide His face from you so that He may hear, for your hands are stained with blood, your fingers are in error."* Yes, my friend, God's hand is strong enough to free us from addiction. It is tedious to hear our prayers. But it is our sin that separates us from God. Jesus can help us when we come to terms with the sin that causes us to separate from God.

My friend, God is more powerful than our addictions and slavery. He can set us free, set us free. The Bible says that when the Son (Jesus) sets you free, you will truly be free. Jesus wants to set you free today. He wants to forgive the past and free each of us from all dependence. He wants to erase past mistakes with His precious blood and make us new creations. God can empower us to overcome temptations that lead us to addiction. Jesus wants us to live a life free from addiction. He wants you to have a quiet life. Let Jesus help you overcome your addiction now.

Declaration

1. I receive strength to overcome each of my harmful addictions.
2. I embrace living the way God outlined in the scriptures.
3. I am strengthened to yield my heart to God's way.

Day 13

MOVING FORWARD

"Not that I have already attained, or am already perfected; but I press on, that I may lay hold of that for which Christ Jesus has also laid hold of me."

Philippians 3:12, NKJV

Permit me to ask you this: How do you want to live your life? Do you want to live a life full of anger and resentment, or do you prefer to live on your own terms? Do you like being drawn to a toxic past or even a challenging present? Did you know that your life, career, and everyday experiences will be much more powerful and focused if you look to the future instead of constantly looking to the past?

I know what my answer would be, and I'm sure yours won't be any different.

Too many people live their lives in the confines of negative experiences. You don't have to be one of them.

It takes energy for positive things to happen. Achieving great things requires concentration and courage. It takes a lot of effort to overcome the many obstacles that stand in your way, and it takes determination to create the life you want. That energy is there to lead you to success, and you shouldn't waste it on meaningless things.

Holding onto a toxic past or present takes too much space and mental and emotional energy. This means you can no longer focus on your present and your future. This will bring you to the point where the past no longer holds you back, and you can build a new life.

The past is over. The events that have happened can no longer hurt you. Understanding this is an essential first step in relaxation. Of course, you can't pretend that there were no painful events in the past, but you can make a choice.

Will you let the past control you, or will you regain control of your future?

People have been telling me stories of how their lives had always changed for the better when they finally got rid of a toxic situation and made the conscious decision to move on.

Leaving the past clears mental and emotional space. It allows you to be open to new opportunities and take risks to create a better life.

1. I receive grace to press onward.
2. I set my face like a flint, staying focused and pursuing my purpose.
3. My strength is renewed to forget my past.

Section Four

FORGIVENESS

Day 14

IS THERE A SECOND CHANCE WITH GOD?

"And the LORD passed before him and proclaimed, "The LORD, the LORD God, merciful and gracious, long-suffering, and abounding in goodness and truth,"

EXODUS 34:6, NKJV

God patiently gives us a second chance, not just one, but multiple. Micah 7:18 says, *"Who is a God like You, pardoning iniquity and passing over the transgression of the remnant of His heritage?"* God enjoys the opportunity to offer second chances and tries not to punish us when we truly ask for forgiveness for our sins (Joel 2:13).

We see this most clearly in the offering of His only begotten Son, Jesus Christ, for the forgiveness of our sins. As the apostle Peter explained, "Who Himself bore our sins in His own body on the tree, that we, having died to sins, might live for righteousness—by whose stripes you were healed."*(1 Peter 2:24)*. Jesus lived a sinless life that we cannot live and died the horrible death we received to give us a second chance to live with God.

I am living proof that your life can be meaningful, exciting, and fulfilling, even if I make a complete mess for a long time. God miraculously saved me.

I encourage you to know that you are serving the Lord of a second chance. The Bible tells many stories about people like me who needed a second chance, and God gave it to them. This teaches us never to underestimate the power of the God we serve and what He does with every mess. No one is outside the power of God's grace.

Maybe you have a past that you are ashamed of. Could it be that you have lived in sin for years and, as a result, feel dirty and stained? Remind yourself that God gives second chances to people with dark pasts.

You see, the enemy will try to hinder and make it difficult for you because of your past. He'd rather you never find forgiveness for this sin, but since you did, he's at least hoping to keep you guilty. But friend, when you have asked God for forgiveness, the past is behind you; He no longer remembers it and wants you to go forward guilt-free, with a new card and a second chance.

A Declaration

1. I receive grace to find my way back into God.
2. I accept the eternal love of God over my life.
3. I solely rely on God's faithfulness to complete His plan over my life.

Day 15

FORGIVING YOURSELF (LET IT GO)

> *"He has not dealt with us according to our sins, Nor punished us according to our iniquities. For as the heavens are high above the earth, So great is His mercy toward those who fear Him;"*
>
> PSALM 103:10-11, NKJV

Almost everyone has one of those moments they can't forgive. You know this: they randomly pop up in your head, tormenting you. The moment when you say something bad about your best friend, and he gets right behind your back; your time at work is full of your boss' faults; you yell at your child just because you had a tough day. Or maybe you cheated, lied, or stole. If the memory of this action makes fun of you, comes at the wrong time, and reminds you of your flaws, whether what you did was really bad or not, you haven't forgiven yourself. And whatever you do, you must do it.

Forgiving yourself is important because you risk committing wrong actions that redefine your self-image if you don't. There's a common misconception that refusing to forgive proves that you're sorrier. But what you're really doing is holding yourself back. We only realize that not forgiving ourselves actually means choosing a less blessed life for ourselves.

Since God is not repaying or relating with us based on the volume of our iniquities, since His love has covered our many errors, we do not need to put ourselves in the bondage of self-guilt. LET GO!

1. I will not limit myself because of my past mistakes.
2. I accept the forgiveness of God over my life.
3. I will not be a victim of self-guilt.

Day 16

FORGIVING OTHERS

"Then Peter came to Him and said, "Lord, how often shall my brother sin against me, and I forgive him? Up to seven times?" Jesus said to him, "I do not say to you, up to seven times, but up to seventy times seven.""

MATTHEW 18:21-22, NKJV

If someone does something wrong in any way, you can rest assured that you will never get over it. Even after your current anger has passed, you can continue to reflect on the betrayal instead of letting it fade into your mind. It's very common to feel that way. But not being able to forgive can really hurt you.

Forgiveness can seem difficult, in part because it is often misunderstood. You can accept that what happened is in the past, admit that people make mistakes, and start cultivating compassion instead.

Forgiving others may seem like a choice, and in some ways, it is a choice, but God is very clear about forgiveness. He has given us specific instructions in many writings, all of which can be summed up in one word - sorry! The Word of God says, *"And whenever you stand praying, if you have anything against anyone, forgive him, that your Father in heaven may also forgive you your trespasses.* (Mark 11:25). *Forgive, and you will be forgiven* (Luke 6:37).

God says it is in our best interest to forgive! He does not talk about what is best for the person to be forgiven. We are the people God is trying to protect. We are the ones who get the most forgiveness, not anyone else. The spirit of un-forgiveness complicates and interferes with our daily walk with God. Forgiving others releases us from anger and allows us to receive the healing we need. The only reason God gives us special instructions is because He doesn't want anything to get in the way of Him and us. God's love for us is beyond our comprehension. Forgiving others saves us from the consequences of living with an unforgiving heart.

Forgiving others does not involve decisions to be considered. God does not classify any sin as more serious than any other, and one sin committed against us does not qualify as justification for forgiveness, and another does not. For example, God doesn't say, "If someone lies to you or steals from you, you should forgive them, but if your child is abused or injured, you can hold them back without mercy." He says to forgive everyone, always and soon.

1. I release everyone that has hurt me in the past.
2. I free my heart from every grudge and bad energy.
3. I receive grace to forgive all those who have wronged me.

Section Five

IDENTITY

Day 17

WHOSE REPORT WILL YOU BELIEVE? (WHAT SOCIETY THINKS OF WOMEN, YOU OR GOD)

"Now they departed and came back to Moses and Aaron and all the congregation of the children of Israel in the Wilderness of Paran, at Kadesh; they brought back word to them and to all the congregation, and showed them the fruit of the land. Then they told him and said: "We went to the land where you sent us. It truly flows with milk and honey, and this is its fruit. Nevertheless, the people who dwell in the land are strong; the cities are fortified and very large; moreover, we saw the descendants of Anak there. The Amalekites dwell in the land of the South; the Hittites, the Jebusites, and the Amorites dwell in the mountains; and the Canaanites dwell by the sea and along the banks of the Jordan." Then Caleb quieted the people before Moses and said, "Let us go up at once and take possession, for we are well able to overcome it. But the men who had gone up with him said, "We are not able to go up against the people, for they are stronger than we." And they gave the children of Israel a bad report of the land which they had spied out, saying, "The land through which we have gone as spies is a land that devours its inhabitants, and all the

> *people whom we saw in it are men of great stature. There we saw the giants (the descendants of Anak came from the giants); and we were like grasshoppers in our own sight, and so we were in their sight."*
>
> NUMBERS 13:26-33, NKJV

Every day we receive "reports" of the news, our experiences, our friends and family, and many other sources. We also receive reports from God's Word that often contradict what others say.

Then we have a choice: should we believe what we hear in nature, or should we believe God's reports?

Who has believed our report? And to whom has the arm of the Lord been revealed? (Isaiah 53:1, NASB)

Women are expected to behave in a certain way, talk in a certain way, and express themselves in a certain "feminine" way. Oh, you can definitely work out at the gym, but you can't look manly or stronger than a man. Oh, you can have a job, but you can't be an engineer or a CEO; that's a man's job. Oh, you can be good at lots of things, but you can never be better than a man.

Our education, what we hear, and the movies we see have all created these expectations. The popular film *Beauty and the Beast* suggests that young girls ignore violence; there is a gentle prince inside, and your job is to kiss the prince and bring him out or kiss the beast and bring the prince out. Women are always expected to be kind, caring, considerate, and patient.

I accept that society is changing now. There is a wave of feminism that has empowered women. Women can work. Women can choose. They are no longer always expected to be stay-at-home moms (at least in America). In fact, men ask their wives to work, but what about the children? People believe that mothers are the best people to take care of children.

Isaiah framed the question for us for all time in the verse above. Therefore, when it comes to our healing, the question still arises, "Who are we going to trust?" We must choose to believe in God's reports.

1. I refuse to listen to the opinions of the world.
2. I choose always to believe the true reports of God.
3. I lean not unto my own understanding, for I will forever trust in God.

Day 18

WHO ARE YOU IN CHRIST? (FINDING SELF)

"Therefore, if anyone is in Christ, he is a new creation; old things have passed away; behold, all things have become new."

— 2 Corinthians 5:17, NKJV

Who am I in Christ? What is my real identity? These are very important questions to our understanding as children of God. You may be asking yourself one of these questions: Who am I? What is my purpose? Why am I here? What should I do with my life? We all have wondered. Don't feel alone or like you are the only one who doubts it. We have a world fighting for our identity.

Who am I in Christ? Your true identity is who you really are. You are identified in Christ. When you accept Him as Lord and Savior in your life, you belong to Him. It becomes your identity!

Understanding our identity in Christ gives us meaning. God has a purpose for each of us, a unique calling for each individual. Our common and most important goal is to become disciples (followers) of Jesus

Christ. Our secondary calling is unique and born of our obedience to the primary calling.

The body of Christ fails when we try to force all women to have a limited understanding of women's roles and responsibilities.

How quickly and easily we forget this with all the distractions, confusion, criticism, and the hustle and bustle of the world. So, if you need this reminder today, you are redeemed by the blood of Christ! It is incomprehensible how great the Father's love is.

The more you agree with God about your identity in Christ, the more your behavior will reflect your God-given identity. I encourage you to learn to see yourself as God sees you. What matters is God's opinion. Accept what God says about you, agree with Him that it's true for you, and be your spiritual person.

Understanding who you are in Christ will give you a solid foundation on which to build your life. Knowing who you are in Jesus is the key to a successful Christian life and a life of purpose.

Your identity does not depend on what others say about you; your identity is in Christ. Hence, no one has the proper definition of you but God.

1. I see myself the way Christ sees me.
2. I am who God says I am.
3. I am the redeemed of the Lord. I am a new creature!

Day 19

WHAT'S THE ESSENCE OF YOUR EXISTENCE?

> "But you *are* a chosen generation, a royal priesthood, a holy nation, His own special people, that you may proclaim the praises of Him who called you out of darkness into His marvelous light; who once *were* not a people but *are* now the people of God, who had not obtained mercy but now have obtained mercy."
>
> — 1 Peter 2:9-10, NKJV

> "You are the light of the world. A city that is set on a hill cannot be hidden. Nor do they light a lamp and put it under a basket, but on a lampstand, and it gives light to all *who are* in the house. Let your light so shine before men, that they may see your good works and glorify your Father in heaven."
>
> — Matthew 5:14-16, NIV

Have you ever thought about the purpose of your life? Some of us live our whole lives trying to understand the meaning of our existence. Often people fail, and others succeed. And then there are those who know the goal but still stray from it.

When you know your purpose in life, you tend to live a more meaningful life than those who don't. You tend to enjoy life to the fullest every day because you know who you are, where you've come from, and where you're going.

Goals can guide life decisions, influence behavior, provide orientation, and create meaning. For some, the goal is related to a vocation - meaningful and rewarding work. For others, their goal is their responsibility to family or friends. Others look for meaning through spirituality or religious beliefs. Some people may find their purpose clear in all these aspects of life.

The goal will be unique to everyone; what you call your own path may be different from someone else's. In addition, your goals may shift and change throughout life in response to changing priorities and fluctuations.

If I may ask, who are you? What on earth do you exist for? Where are you? Where are you going to? Is there a defined destination of where you're going? Or do you live your life to chance? Know this, every woman who made a mark here on earth fulfilled a purpose. Have you discovered yours?

1. Step out of the table now and pause for a minute; then ask yourself, who am I? Can you simply answer I am the light of the world!
2. I am a city set on a hill. I can't be hidden.
3. I am chosen. I am God's special possession.

Section Six
FREEDOM

Day 20

NO MORE CONDEMNATION

"There is therefore, now no condemnation to them which are in Christ Jesus, who walk not after the flesh, but after the Spirit. For the law of the Spirit of life in Christ Jesus hath made me free from the law of sin and death."

— ROMANS 8:1-2, KJV

"No condemnation" in courtroom language means not being convicted or found guilty of the charge. By the grace of God, those who believe in Jesus Christ will not face God's judgment. "We passed from death into life" (1 John 3:14).

However, "no condemnation" implies more than deliverance on the Day of Judgment. In Romans 8:1, the apostle Paul spoke in the present tense, as the word *now* shows. So also pay attention to the word that leads the reader to the earlier passage in Romans 7:21-25. In Romans 7, Paul describes his struggle against sinful nature - a struggle that every believer experiences. Paul wrote, *"I want to do good, but evil is with me"* and *"How wretched I am!"* Paul expresses his hatred for the sinful nature that continues to struggle against his new nature in Christ - Paul hates the sin he has committed, but he is also grateful to have been freed from the bondage of sin. He now has the ability to do good because Christ saved him (Romans 7:25).

Paul goes a step further in Romans 8 when he teaches a believer not only to be free from bondage to sin but also to be free from the internal emotions and thoughts that tend to make a Christian feel condemned when they sin. We are not under the condemnation of the law because Jesus perfectly fulfills the expectations of the law. Because believers are in Christ, they rejoice in being considered righteous only because Christ is righteous (Philippians 3:9).

Paul encourages us not to fear judgment because we can come to God as our loving and forgiving Father (Romans 8:15-16). Christians who live in shame and guilt because of past failures need not be punished when they *"Forget what is behind them and look for what is to come"* (Philippians 3:13). Fear can paralyze, *"But perfect love casts out fear"* (1 John 4:18). As Christians, we must understand that our justification lies in Christ alone, in His finished work on the cross, not in what we do or do not do (Romans 3:28). Believers can find comfort in knowing that we have been accepted into God's own family and become heirs of God and joint-heirs with Christ. Nothing can separate us *"from the love of God which is in Christ Jesus."*

Declaration

1. I am free from my past mistakes and self-guilt.
2. The blood of Jesus has made a new way for me.
3. The righteousness of Christ has been imputed on me. I am the righteousness of God.

Day 21

NO MORE LIMITATIONS

"For God has not given us a spirit of fear, but of power and of love and of a sound mind."

2 Timothy 1:7, NKJV

We have all experienced limitations or stagnation at some point in our lives. It is not strange or new. The weird thing is sitting around and doing nothing. Stagnation means having what it takes to move forward, but you still can't make progress. For example, rich and beautiful but still not married, highly qualified but unable to find a good job, perfect for having children, but unable to give birth. Limitations do not allow you to maximize your potential.

Fear can also limit a Christian from reaching or maximizing his potential. Mind Restriction (thinking) also happens. In Numbers 13, when the children of Israel were spying on the earth, 10 out of 12 were restricted in their minds and were considered locusts. Thank goodness for Joshua and Caleb for not being negative or limited.

Free your mind from limitations. Your chances in life and your journey to greatness begin with a positive mindset. *"Whatever things are true, whatever things are noble, whatever things are just, whatever things are pure, whatever things are lovely, whatever things are of good report, if there is any virtue and if there is anything praiseworthy—meditate on these things." (Philippians 4:8)*

To remove a sheet of paper from the table, you simply blow air from your mouth. Moving the dictionary may take a little pushing by hand, but to move the generator or a big installation, you will need a crane or heavy machinery.

To stop being restricted, you need a "heavy machine" called the HOLY SPIRIT. You may have done everything, but you will make great PROGRESS if you do it by faith. You have to use the power of the HOLY SPIRIT.

1. My mind is renewed for greater possibilities.
2. I am unstoppable. I am more than a conqueror.
3. I receive the power of the Holy Ghost to do all things through Christ.

Day 22

LAUNCH THE WOMAN IN YOU

"A gracious woman retains honor."
Proverbs 11:16a, NKJV

In today's time, we're constantly met with an onslaught of so many different opinions of what it means to be a woman. I wish we could have time to study every woman in the Bible. I believe learning about Mary, Sarah and Hannah will be so insightful and eye-opening.

Are women independently strong and better than men? Are women weak or giving up their lives if they want to be wives and mothers? Are women given a beautiful gift in Jesus Christ to live?

Sure, the beautiful women we looked to in the Bible were imperfect, just like you and me. But dear lady, the reason why we looked to a few of the Bible's most beautiful women is that they show glimpses of the character traits, practices, and postures that God desires for His beautiful daughters to have.

If you've not learned anything from this whole devotional, I pray you learn that God's design for women is beautiful, worthwhile, weighty, and oh-so needed.

As we seek to be stronger and become more effective women for God's kingdom, there are some traits we need to study and soak in these truths and begin to unleash the awesomeness of womanhood in us.

You need to unleash the woman in you by; seeking and putting God first, showing your true beauty, being humble, serving the Lord and others with a meek and loving heart, treasuring the beautiful role God has given you, being brave and bold with God's Word and your gifts.

1. I am beautifully and fearfully made by the maker of Heaven and Earth.
2. I am an embodiment of beauty, glory, and honor.
3. I unleash every treasure of God in me for my world to see.

Day 23

LAUNCH YOUR POTENTIAL

"Meditate on these things; give yourself entirely to them, that your progress may be evident to all."

1 Timothy 4:15, NKJV

We all have the same number of hours in a day. But when we think about it, why do some people succeed while others are disappointed? There's something we're missing or doing nothing about. We also gain skills and talents that we need to improve and develop. If we can only bring out the hidden potential within us, we can surely achieve many things and become successful in life.

Have you ever asked yourself, "Am I quite happy and content with the life I have now?"

Success doesn't come with time. You have to work hard for it.

We often confine ourselves to a narrow space and leave our abilities and talents unrevealed. This keeps us trapped in insecurity, which leads to low self-esteem and self-confidence. We face limited possibilities. You need to constantly remind yourself that there will never be any significant life changes in your comfort zone. If you want true success, you must strengthen and develop yourself with your best self. Often it takes courage and determination to achieve the goal. Your potential, skills, and talents are the keys to your core growth. Believe it or not, you can achieve more and be better than you think.

Everyone has a talent, and many people ignore it, and very few people take advantage of that talent and use it. There is something specific and unique to everyone. Not every star is designed to be visible. Everyone is an expert in their field. Everyone here is a star. We are a megastar of the church.

It is important to know that God does not have to anoint us just to preach. He anoints people in their profession.

Two things make some people more successful than others: character and competence.

1. I refuse to be an unprofitable servant. I will utilize my potential.
2. I step out of my comfort zone, and I maximize every God-given ability in me.
3. I will shine my light for all to see.

Day 24

LAUNCH THE LEADER IN YOU

> *"Village life ceased, it ceased in Israel, until I,
> Deborah, arose, arose a mother in Israel."*
>
> JUDGES 5:7, NKJV

Now is the time to rise together, help each other and find common ground in our work. Men are very good at relating to one another, which can sometimes lead to unconscious prejudice. Women need the same support to feel recognized and valued. We must not deviate from the qualities that make us clearly feminine but understand that being ourselves is more important.

Women struggle for advancement in the ladder and currently occupy only about a third of all management positions. Often the problem is that they are not given the opportunities they need to grow and develop. Therefore, more women than men said they planned to leave their current employer in search of their next job.

As ladies of great character, we need to begin a conscious movement of rising to our leadership mandate and role. In the scripture, we saw how Deborah made the bold statement, *"Until I, Deborah arose."* That is a bold statement.

The nation of Israel was not experiencing peace; they were in confusion until Deborah rose to her mandate as a mother and a voice in Israel. This is God's own nation with a history of men as past leaders. This clearly shows that you can also rise up the ladder of leadership in your country no matter what the history or the norm says.

1. I will rise and climb the ladder of leadership in my environment.
2. I am a voice and a light to my generation.
3. I will no longer be silenced or relegated to the background.

Day 25

REACH FOR THE STARS

"Seest thou a man diligent in his business? He shall stand before kings; he shall not stand before mean men."

Proverbs 22:29, KJV

Everyone has a dream. No matter what dreams you are trying to pursue, regardless of whether it is to save humanity, to overcome poverty, or to end hunger, the truth is that your dreams matter.

The world is full of paradoxes. One of the biggest is the tradeoff between having high and low expectations. It is a prerequisite to becoming your best self. On the one hand, we need to expect to win at life; otherwise, what is the point of even trying? But on the other hand, also, we can't be discouraged when we lose out on dreams.

I have started on certain businesses that didn't meet my expectations in my life's journey, just like some of you. Yes! It's all part of your success story. Each time you go through tough times, just like me, always keep the vision alive.

Naturally, you'll get to a point where you feel you couldn't do it on your own. Don't let those high expectations make you give up. For me, I'm glad I kept going and stayed positive.

The problem is not whether you fail or not. It's about what you want to do about it? Do you want to stop there? Cry and moan, saying, "Why does this always happen to me?" We all know that is not helpful. Instead, we must be indifferent to outcomes and pursue more!

But still, I do think you must be fired up to expect to win at everything in life: your career, relationships, and money. Aim high and do everything in your control to become your best self. That's the most useful way to spend your time.

1. I say no to mediocrity. I consciously aim for the best.
2. My success today is just a stepping stone to greater success tomorrow.
3. I begin to make global impacts. I am no longer restrained to my locality.

Section Seven

THE LOVE OF GOD

Day 26

HOW DEEP IS THE FATHER'S LOVE?

> *"Behold what manner of love the Father has bestowed on us, that we should be called children of God! Therefore the world does not know us because it did not know Him."*
>
> — 1 JOHN 3:1, NKJV

There is no power stronger than the love Heavenly Father feels for us, His children. His love can move mountains, stop the raging seas, heal broken bones and hearts, change lives, and set free those held captive by sin and shame. His love for you and me was so great that He sent His only Son to die so we could live through Him. And in John 17:25-26, Jesus makes an inexplicable statement about the depth of God's love for us.

With Christ's death, the barrier between us and our relationship with God is torn in two. God's wrath rejoices over Jesus' death, and now we can experience the full depths of His love. Through Christ, we are made new so that in the end, we can walk in unhindered fellowship and union with the God of the perfect world.

God loves you only because He loves you. You don't have to work for His affection. You don't have to wake up before God can pour out His love on you. In the story of the prodigal son, the father ran to his son before anything was fixed. He didn't know his son was there to apologize. He didn't care. He just wanted to love his son. Your Heavenly Father feels the same way about you. He misses loving you wherever you are, just the way you are. He longs to fill you with love to the brim. He longs for us to experience that love and oneness, just as Jesus did when he walked the earth.

1. I am deeply loved by God, and I will reciprocate His love.
2. I consciously walk in the light of His love.
3. His constant banner over me is love.

Day 27

GOD'S LOVE NEVER FAILS

> *"It is of the Lord's mercies that we are not consumed, because His compassions fail not. They are new every morning: great is thy faithfulness."*
> — Lamentations 3:22-23, KJV

> *"Though the mountains be shaken, and the hills be removed, yet my unfailing love for you will not be shaken nor my covenant of peace be removed, says the Lord, who has compassion on you."*
> — Isaiah 54:10, NIV

What lasts forever? It may be difficult for you to find something that fits this description. But today, we know one thing that is endless: God's love.

When children fail or do things they shouldn't, parents can become frustrated and even discipline their children, but a good parent's love for their child never changes, rejects, or fails because the love of a mother or father is unconditional. Parents love their children because they have them.

The same is true of us and our relationship with God the Father. He loves us because we are His. There is nothing we can do to change that fact.

In Hosea 11, we see how God loved His children Israel even when they turned away from Him. As long as Israel failed, God's love for them never failed. God is a loving Father who expects good gifts for His children. His love is unconditional. God's love is not based on what Israel did or didn't do; it is based on their status as His children. Nothing can change God's love for you.

You may wonder how God can still love you, but your position as His child has not changed. His love for you is still the same. You may think that God can never love you for what you did. God's love is not based on what you did but on what Jesus did on the cross.

God's love for you is not based on your condition but on your position as His child. You may fail in your life, but God's love for you will never fail.

1. I embrace the never-failing love of God.
2. I am eternally loved by God through His sure mercies.
3. I walk daily in the newness of His compassion towards me.

Day 28

HIS BANNER OVER YOU IS LOVE

"I am a rose of Sharon, a lily of the valleys. As a lily among brambles, so is my love among the young women. As an apple tree among the trees of the forest, so is my beloved among the young men. With great delight I sat in his shadow, and his fruit was sweet to my taste. He brought me to the banqueting house, and his banner over me was love. Sustain me with raisins; refresh me with apples, for I am sick with love."

— Song of Solomon 2:1-5, ESV —

This passage of the Song of Solomon is actually a romance between two people in love seeking intimacy with each other, but it serves as an allegory of God's relationship with us, His loved ones. I remember studying Solomon 2:4 as a child, so I've known this verse for a long time. But lately, God has done a really great thing in me. He increased my curiosity to pause and ask about popular Bible verses and concepts I've known all my life, "What does this really mean?"

Whether we realize it or not, our existence in this world is not accidental or meaningless; God created us and placed us in this world to serve His unique purpose in our lives. We cannot know our purpose in life outside of God, and a life lived outside of God is meaningless. For me personally, God has been the focus of my entire life since I started a relationship with Him. My intention to exist in the world did not arise outside of Him or make sense without Him.

Simply being a light in this dark world is walking in love and sharing the peace, love, and fulfillment that I find through a personal relationship with God.

I have been private in times past about my personal beliefs because, as I have studied, it makes you feel weird when you're free and often speak about His faith. Also, because of the diversity of people with different beliefs, you are more likely to violate someone's religious sensibilities.

This journey to gain a deeper understanding of Solomon 2:4 made me realize that God claims us, proudly says we belong to Him, and loudly declares, "I love you!" Our whole life is about us. Talk about yourself. God supports and carries you throughout your life. Like everyone else, God wants His love to be appreciated, reciprocated, and prioritized.

1. I will proclaim the love of God over my life everywhere.
2. I am the beloved of God. God is proud of me.
3. I will radiate the love of God to everyone around me.

Day 29

GOD'S LOVE IS PATIENT

"The Lord Is Not Slow To Fulfill His Promise As Some Count Slowness, But Is Patient Toward You, Not Wishing That Any Should Perish, But That All Should Reach Repentance."

— 2 Peter 3:9, Esv

"But You, O Lord, Are A God Merciful And Gracious; Slow To Anger And Abounding In Steadfast Love And Faithfulness."

— Psalm 86:15, Esv

"And Count The Patience Of Our Lord As Salvation, Just As Our Beloved Brother Paul Also Wrote To You According To The Wisdom Given Him."

— 2 Peter 3:15, Esv

How do you know when someone really loves you? The world is looking for love. Everyone wants to know something about love. God says in 1 Corinthians 13:4: *"Love is long-suffering."* The first thing God said about love was patience. Cooking takes a long time.

The first two statements of 1 Corinthians 13:4 in the Greek text say "love" is patient and "love" is kind. Then the word "love" is only repeated in verse 8 when it says, *"Love never fails."* That means there are two definitions of love: patience and kindness. The next eight are negative. Did you see that? Negative is arranged in Greek grammar to describe patience and kindness. For example, if you are patient, you will not be jealous. You don't show off; you don't bloat. Do not act violently, think evil, or provoke yourself. These things are negative and describe the two qualities of love, namely patience and kindness. And the first thing God is telling you is that love is patience.

Look, when someone says, "I love you," you don't know if they really love you or not. Did you know that? You do not know. Look, it's always good to hear the words. Someone comes and says, "I love you so much." You can say to yourself, "Okay, I can think of a few reasons why that is." But if you don't know why someone says, "Oh, I love you so much," you're not going to say, "Well, I see why you think that." I mean, you don't know what to say. But you'll see if it's true in time, especially if you're not performing well. Especially when you don't live up to the expectations of the person who says, "I love you."

Now we will find out whether you have God's love or not. The only kind of love that sustains, builds, encourages you, and takes you to another day is love that is always there. Love is patient. That means there is reason to be angry. Have you noticed that there are people who don't deserve your "I love you" words? Do you understand that? In fact, you don't deserve it either.

When we talk about God's patience, we mean that He is in control of His perfect and sovereign plan. This calms His just anger and allows forgiveness, and it marks His great love.

God's patience is long. God's patience is amazing. He, deeply offended by every sin, chose to show great patience, and we see that patience is manifested in the Old and New Testaments and in the lives of people today.

God is "slow to anger" and very patient but "will not leave the guilty unpunished." In other words, God will always punish evil, but on His own schedule. The concept of "slow to anger" means He shows self-control. In some versions, the word for Christ's patience in 2 Thessalonians 3:5 is "endurance," but elsewhere, it is translated as "patient perseverance."

God can instigate immediate punishment for sin as in Ananias and Sapphira, or in other cases, He can indicate a suspended or long-suffering punishment until His sovereign purpose is fulfilled.

We must not confuse God's patience with His grace. A person who continues to have a sinful habit without being immediately judged may mistakenly think that there will be no consequences. While God is very patient, it is foolish to assume that there will be no day of vengeance.

God's silence on sin is not synonymous with approval, and toying with God is unwise because He never loses. His intentions were not thwarted by those who mocked or opposed Him. His sovereign goal will always prevail.

1. I will not take the patience of God for granted.
2. I embrace the saving grace and the patient love of God.
3. I trust in the wisdom of God to fulfill His promises in due time.

Day 30

GOD'S LOVE IS EVERLASTING

"What then shall we say to these things? If God is for us, who can be against us? He who did not spare His own Son, but delivered Him up for us all, how shall He not with Him also freely give us all things?"

— ROMANS 8:31-32, KJV —

"The LORD has appeared of old to me, saying:
"Yes, I have loved you with an everlasting love;
Therefore with loving kindness, I have drawn you."

— JEREMIAH 31:3, NKJV —

God is love. His love is from everlasting to everlasting. He showed us love through His son Jesus Christ. It's too unfortunate many of us don't appreciate the miracle of God's love. God's love never loses its effectiveness. This love is the most amazing and wonderful thing that has ever existed. This love of God in Jesus Christ for His church is eternal love. It was a love so deep in His heart. It exists forever and ever. That love is sacrificial. We read how Christ loved the church and gave Him up for it. He gave Himself to the cross, to torment, to suffering, to endure our eternal hell. That love is a love that saves. It is the love through which He draws us to Himself. Out of His loving-kindness, said Jeremiah, God draws us.

God's love brings help. God does not love without the ability to bring the object of His love to Himself. Oh, God's love is a mighty power. Everything must give way to this love. In love, He brought the church to Him. And that love is true love. He's not like a fickle man. So, He loved the church. And in this love, He cleansed the church from all its sins and made it righteous and pure in the Son. Through His love, He gives the Holy Spirit through which we repent.

And through all these things, He brings us into the covenant. Jesus Christ loves His church. He loves me. He loves everyone brought to Him by grace. He loves the repentant believer. Say this, repentant believers, "The Son of God loves me."

Some people have turned away from God through sin, only to come back later to seek forgiveness. Take, for example, how God freed the Israelites from slavery in Egypt. As free as they became, they struggled to keep their faith in God alive.

Despite their changing beliefs, God still loves them. He kept His promise from generation to generation that they would inherit the Promised Land. Although not everyone lived to see the fulfillment of that promise, God keeps His Word to His people.

Another show of God's everlasting love is when non-believers, like Paul, found salvation. Paul, who once persecuted Christians, became the one who preached the gospel. Even though he didn't start as one of God's people, he became one. This turn in his story reflects the kind of love God shows to His people by continually accepting us with open arms wherever we are on our journey of faith.

When these examples reflect God's eternal love, we can be sure that God's love will endure for generations. His love is full of forgiveness. God is ready to make us His when we are ready for Him.

God wants nothing more than to accept us and redeem us to be better people. God's love is eternal. Unconditional in nature. No matter how we define God's love, we cannot ignore its eternal quality.

No matter what we have done or where we are on our journey of faith, God wants to love us. Whether we are just starting to believe or still have doubts, God is ready and willing to embrace us with His eternal love.

1. I will not forget the eternal love of God that transcends generations.
2. I am loved by God unconditionally, not by my works, but by His Grace.
3. I embrace the open arms of God.

CONCLUSION

The era when women get the least in society is passed. The era when women had no voice and were relegated and reduced to the kitchen is passed. The era when women were denied key leadership positions is passed. The era when women kept silent in the church to only ask their husbands questions at home is passed. The era when women waited for men before spending money is passed. Womanhood has evolved over time.

We're in the era of grace and power. The female folks are not exempt. Seriously, we must rise to fulfill destiny. Our lives must be exemplary. In the body of Christ, we must begin to impact lives as we allow Christ to impact us too. We must begin to see beyond the challenges we face. We must begin to see beyond societal rejection and discrimination. For we can do all things through Christ who gives us strengthens us (Philippians 4:13).

This should serve as a wake-up call for you to open up your world and begin to desire a personal and more intimate relationship with God.

Your relevance as a woman is a function of your intimacy with God and the Holy Spirit. How deep is your relationship with Him? There will never be a relationship in your life that's more important than the one you have with God in Christ. You could say that you're a friend of the president or prime minister of your country, or perhaps even the heads of all states, yet nothing compares to being the friend of the

Creator of the universe. Your relationship with God is more important than any other relationship you'll ever have in life.

As women who follow Jesus, we know the truth. We also have the opportunity to let the glory of this truth shine through our lives. Where reason fails us, we can exemplify God's way with our living. The abundance of joy, fulfillment, eternal heritage, and His glory in our lives will bear witness to God's good plan.

God poured His incomprehensible grace and power into both males and females. God, in His goodness and love, bestowed a glorious and honored mothering nature upon women. When we embrace our innate womanhood, we will experience fulfillment. There is a great depth, beauty, and creative possibility within this design!

Women of God: Rise up! Unleash your uniqueness. Unleash your potential.

Women of God: Rise up! Adorn yourselves with the unfading beauty of a God's glory.

Women of God: Rise up! Take up the responsibility to lift others up.

Women of God: Rise up! Be who God made you to be!

***The radiance and influence of a woman who
fears the Lord is truly limitless.***

www.ingramcontent.com/pod-product-compliance
Lightning Source LLC
Chambersburg PA
CBHW030914080526
44589CB00010B/295